INCLUSIVE READERS
SERIES

Libby Martin

Teachers' Book

Maggie Walker
Val Davis
Ann Berger

David Fulton Publishers
London

David Fulton Publishers Ltd
Ormond House
26–27 Boswell Street
London WC1N 3JZ

First published in Great Britain in 2002 by David Fulton Publishers Ltd

Copyright © 2002 Maggie Walker, Val Davis, Ann Berger
Illustrations © 2002 Sarah Wimperis of Gordon-Cameron Illustration
Writing with Symbols © 2002 Widgit Software

British Library Cataloguing in Publication Data
A catalogue record is available from the British Library.

ISBN: 1-85346-887-8

The materials in this publication may be photocopied only for use within the purchasing organisation. Otherwise, all rights reserved. No part of this publication may be reproduced, stored in a retrieval system or transmitted in any form or by any means, electronic, mechanical, photocopying, recording or otherwise, without the prior permission of the publisher.

Designed and typeset by Kenneth Burnley, Wirral, Cheshire
Printed and bound in Great Britain by Bell and Bain Ltd, Glasgow

Contents

Introduction	v
Weekly plan for each level from P1–2C	1
Suggestions for further activities	4
List of items for a multisensory pack	7
Symbols	8
Word strips	10

Two differentiated versions of the text with symbols for pupils working at:
    levels P5–P6
    levels P7–1C

Differentiated version of the text for pupils working at levels 1B–2C

Ten examples of resource sheets for use with the suggested activities:

Resource Sheet 1: My morning	45
Resource Sheet 2: Alphabetical order	46
Resource Sheet 3: Punctuation	47
Resource Sheet 4: Past tense words	48
Resource Sheet 5: Letter patterns	49
Resource Sheet 6: Opposites	50
Resource Sheet 7: Writing a letter	51
Resource Sheet 8: Getting dressed	52
Resource Sheet 9: Libby Martin	53
Resource Sheet 10: Libby and Sam	54

Note: All of these resources may be photocopied, cut out and laminated as required.

Introduction

Pupils who are at the early stages of acquiring literacy skills need motivating texts to support their learning. The Inclusive Readers series of books is designed to provide this. It is based on the scheme of work developed by Bristol Schools, which has been published in the second edition of *Implementing the Literacy Hour for Pupils with Learning Difficulties* (David Fulton 2001).

The big books include fiction, non-fiction styles and poetry, and each individual book focuses on one specific genre that should be covered in Key Stage 2. Some of the texts are also suitable for use with pupils in Years 7 and 8. In the centre of each big book is a pull-out section, which features characters and objects from the texts that can be cut out and laminated, and used to support multisensory teaching strategies. Each Teachers' Book includes a wide range of activities that can be used with pupils to reinforce their understanding of the text and the development of word and sentence level skills. They are linked to the Key Stage 1 objectives in the National Literacy Strategy but designed to be appropriate for pupils between 7 and 12 years of age.

The Teachers' Book also includes three differentiated texts based on the big book, which are designed to be used during guided reading work. They are produced at three levels linked to the revised P scales. The P5–P6 and P7–1C books have symbols as well as words to reinforce reading skills. The level 1B–2C books have only words. Each of these differentiated texts is illustrated with black and white versions of the pictures from the big book, and is fully photocopiable for individual use, and also for the use of parents to support pupils at home.

We have worked closely with Widgit Software to develop appropriate symbols for certain key words. These symbols can be copied and used in other contexts to reinforce the learning. They are also available for Writing with Symbols.

This story shows a day in the life of Libby, who does everything slowly and methodically. It is written around the different sorts of lists and instructions which get her through her day. The questions to the reader encourage children to think about the different ways they carry out tasks in their everyday life, and to consider when the right order matters, and when it doesn't.

National Literacy Strategy

Weekly Plan

Class _____ Teacher _____ Date _____

	Whole class shared reading and writing	**Whole class phonics, spelling, vocabulary and grammar**	**Guided group tasks P1–P2**	**Guided group tasks P3–P4**	**Plenary**
Mon	LIBBY MARTIN	Find out from parents/carers what the morning routine is for each pupil. Obtain photos if possible. Share with pupils	Play with some morning routine objects, such as hairbrush, toothbrush, pyjamas	Make a timetable of each pupil's morning routine using pictures and symbols	Can pupils follow a routine, knowing what happens next?
Tues		Talk about breakfast. Taste some breakfast cereals	Make a chocolate banana sandwich to share at break time	Make a collage with packages of breakfast cereals, bread bags, etc.	How do pupils indicate food likes and dislikes?
Wed		Talk about music lessons at school	Play with a selection of shakers	Decorate a shaker	Can pupils manipulate toys?
Thur		Watch part of a *Postman Pat* video or the Watch video about letters	Look inside some big envelopes for a surprise	Open some envelopes to see what's inside or put some letters in envelopes	Do pupils understand object permanence?
Fri	Look at several books. Put favourites in a special place to read later		Shared reading. Touch or hold the book carefully, turn pages, etc.	Shared reading. Point to pictures as asked	Are pupils interested in books and stories?

National Literacy Strategy

Weekly Plan

Class _____ Teacher _____ Date _____

	Whole class shared reading and writing	**Whole class phonics, spelling, vocabulary and grammar**	**Guided group tasks P5–P6**	**Guided group tasks P7–P8**	**Plenary**
Mon	LIBBY MARTIN	Talk about Libby Martin. What kind of person is she?	Draw a picture of yourself getting up in the morning. Write a caption	Fold a piece of paper into quarters. In each space draw something you do in the morning. Write a caption for each	Can pupils make a judgement about characters in books?
Tues	Answer some of the questions posed in the book		Dramatise some parts of the story. Show your performance to the rest of the group	Make a list of all the people in this book. Write one word to describe each one	What type of questions can pupils answer about the story?
Wed		Discuss the layout of one of the pages in the book. Is it the same as other books you know?	Take a list of ingredients and put them in alphabetical order	Adult photocopies and cuts out a set of instructions. Pupils put them in the correct order	Can pupils sequence: instructions? in alphabetical order?
Thur	Look at some recipe books		Make a list of things you need for a chocolate banana sandwich	Write a recipe for a favourite sandwich	Do pupils understand the written structure of a recipe?
Fri		Talk about the good qualities in each pupil in the group	Draw a picture of your friend. Say why you like him/her	Draw a picture of your favourite person. Write why you like him/her	Can pupils join in a discussion with the group?

National Literacy Strategy

Weekly Plan

Class _____ Teacher _____ Date _____

	Whole class shared reading and writing	**Whole class phonics, spelling, vocabulary and grammar**	**Guided group tasks 1C–1A**	**Guided group tasks 2C–2A**	**Plenary**
Mon	LIBBY MARTIN	Talk about pupils' daily routines. Do they do the same things every day, like Libby?	Make a list of things you do every morning	Make a little book with drawings and writing about your daily morning routine	How many words can pupils spell independently?
Tues		Discuss what makes instructions different from other kinds of writing	Look at a recipe book. How is it the same as/different from the recipe for chocolate banana sandwiches?	Write some instructions for getting drinks ready for your group	Can pupils explain what instructions are?
Wed	Talk about why some words in the book are written in capital letters		Draw and write about something you did yesterday	Write some instructions for getting ready for PE. Now write them again as if you did it yesterday. Compare	Do pupils understand about past and present tense?
Thur		Look at where full stops and capital letters are in the book. Is the book following the usual rules?	Write a sentence about Libby and put in the capital letters and full stop	Write some sentences about Libby and put in as much punctuation as you can	Are pupils using capital letters accurately?
Fri		Discuss Libby's relationship with her dad	Draw your dad (or mum) and describe him (or her)	Write about something you did with your dad that you liked	Can pupils empathise with characters in books?

National Literacy Strategy

Suggestions for further activities

Text: *Libby Martin*

P1–P2

- Make a class timetable using objects of reference, pictures and/or symbols
- Dress a doll together. Talk about each item of clothing referring to the pupils' clothing
- Walk to the post box and post a letter
- Work on the identification of the pupils' own coat and bag
- Make a collection of things related to post, e.g. envelopes, stamps, parcels, address book, toy post box
- Share a picture related to the story, e.g. cooking, writing a letter, getting dressed

P3–P4

- Make up a song like:

    'First I put my socks on, my socks on, my socks on,

    First I put my socks on

    When I'm getting dressed'
- Make a class timetable using objects of reference, pictures and/or symbols
- Invite a postman to come to class and talk about his job
- Ask the school secretary or head teacher to open the school post in the classroom. Pupils could help
- Brush a doll's hair, clean its teeth and dress it in pyjamas
- Talk about bedtime routines
- Mash bananas with a fork and then eat them
- Adult prepares photocopied pictures of a shaker. Pupils colour or design a pattern
- Stick 'stamps' in the top right corner of envelopes
- Draw a picture of your friend. Ask him/her to help you to write their name underneath

P5–P6

- Use the BBC IT programme 'Dress'
- Compose some music using shakers
- Make a trail with string on pieces of paper from the classroom to the hall and then ask another person to follow it
- Take some photographs of the sequence of posting a letter or making a sandwich. Pupils put them in order
- Write a letter to a friend
- Listen to some music and add an accompaniment with shakers

P7–P8

- Draw pictures of all the drinks that the pupils in your group have for breakfast and write the name of each underneath
- Make a shaker following Libby and Sam's instructions
- Address an envelope to yourself
- Photocopy one of the pages from the book. Carefully copy over any of the words you can read or any words that begin with the same letter as your name
- Make a pattern of capital and lower-case letters, e.g. LILILILILILI
- Discuss the meaning of 'a creature of habit'
- Set up a class post box. Write a simple letter to each pupil over several days. Help them read it when they find it
- Discuss which sets of instructions in the book are easiest to follow. Which are hardest?

1C–1B

- Try doing something differently, like writing with the other hand, brushing your hair with the other hand or sitting on a chair the other way around
- Adult makes a list of words from the text in random order. Pupils put the words in alphabetical order
- Ask everyone in your group what is their favourite kind of sandwich and then make a list
- Look at some TV magazines. Make a list of your three favourite programmes
- Choose your favourite recipe from a cookery book. Explain to your friend why you think you would like it

1A–2C

- Examine the questions in the text. Notice the question marks. Write some questions and add question marks
- Make a list of question words
- Write some instructions for classroom jobs like watering plants, stacking chairs, tidying up toys, and stick them up around the classroom
- Choose some words from the text that have 'opposites', e.g. slowly, on, up, same, over. Make a list and put the opposite word beside each one
- Adult writes instructions for some simple tasks, e.g. brushing teeth, laying the table, opening a bottle of juice, but misses out the last one. Pupils complete the instructions
- Write a class recipe together for a person that everyone knows but who is not in your class
- Make a shopping list of things to make a chocolate banana sandwich and then go and buy them

Multisensory pack

Doll with pyjamas, pants, vest, trousers, T-shirt, sweatshirt, socks, shoes

Bread

Chocolate spread

Bananas

Toaster

Selection of shakers

Symbols

Libby

dad

school

Sam

gets up

dressed

Symbols

breakfast

like(s)

shaker

home

read

they

Word strips

List 1

and	dad
the	get(s)
said	go
a	you
are	to
at	I
like(s)	they
up	come(s)

Word strips

List 2

got	what
do	made
good	when
first	her
school	home
then	very
make	do

Word strips

Context words and names

Libby	Sam
dressed	breakfast
shaker	slowly
socks	bread
trousers	banana
shirt	chocolate
bottle	paper
peas	things

Differentiated versions of the text

On the following pages you will find three differentiated versions of the story *Libby Martin*, for use with individual pupils working at the following levels:

The version for pupils working at levels P5–6 uses the following key words:

HF words List 1	dad get(s) up and go to like(s)
List 2	her school home
Context words	dressed
Names	Libby('s) Sam

The version for pupils working at levels P7–1C uses the following key words:

HF words List 1	get(s) up dad a and go to they like(s) come(s)
List 2	her make school home
Context words	dressed breakfast shaker
Names	Libby('s) Sam('s)

The version for pupils working at levels 1B–2C uses the following key words:

HF words List 1	get up dad at and a you are I like said the
List 2	got first then made school good do very make
Context words	slowly dressed socks trousers shirt breakfast bread banana chocolate shaker bottle peas paper things
Names	Libby Sam

Each of these texts can be photocopied and made into individual books. We have also included a black and white version of the cover of the story book which can be copied, laminated and used for individual book covers.

Libby Martin

Maggie Walker

Illustrated by Sarah Wimperis

Text for pupils working at levels P5–6

Libby gets up.

Libby gets dressed.

Libby and her dad.

Libby and Sam go to school.

Libby and Sam like school.

 L  S

Libby and Sam go home.

Libby and her dad go home.

Libby likes her dad.

Libby's dad likes her.

Libby Martin

Maggie Walker

Illustrated by Sarah Wimperis

Text for pupils working at levels P7–1C

Libby gets up.

Libby gets dressed.

 Libby and her dad

 make breakfast.

Libby and Sam go to school.

They like school.

They make a shaker.

Libby and Sam go to

Sam's home.

Dad comes to get Libby.

They go home.

Libby's dad likes Libby.

Libby likes her dad.

 Libby.

Libby Martin

Maggie Walker

Illustrated by Sarah Wimperis

Text for pupils working at levels 1B–2C

'Libby, get up.
Libby, get up!
LIBBY, GET UP!' said dad.

Libby got up, slowly.

Libby got dressed, slowly.

First the socks,
then the trousers,
then the shirt.

Libby made breakfast, slowly.

First the bread,
then the banana,
then the chocolate.

At school, Libby and Sam made a shaker, slowly.

First the bottle,
then the peas,
then the paper.

'You are very good, Libby,' said her dad.
'You make a good banana and chocolate breakfast.
You make a good shaker.
You do things slowly.
I like you, Libby,' said dad.
'I like you, dad,' said Libby.

My morning

RESOURCE SHEET 1

Name _____

In each space draw something you do in the morning. You could write captions for your pictures.

My morning

45

Alphabetical order

RESOURCE SHEET 2

Name _____

Here are the things you need to make a chocolate banana sandwich. Put them in alphabetical order:

banana   chocolate spread   bread

toaster   knife

Now do the same for the things you need to make a shaker:

plastic bottle   dried peas   paper

sellotape   felt-tips

Punctuation

RESOURCE SHEET 3

Name _____

Punctuate these sentences. You can use capital letters, full stops and question marks.

1. libby did the same things every day

2. what do you do when you get up

3. dad always had a smile for libby in the morning

4. what do you want for breakfast libby

5. did sam put peas or beans in his shaker

6. did you buy a sticky cake sam

7. you are a brilliant reader libby martin

8. what is the recipe to make you

9. at 8 oclock she went to bed as usual

10. is sam libbys friend

Past tense words

RESOURCE SHEET 4

Name _____

Change these words into past tense:

sing	
play	
jump	
write	
sleep	
stick	
run	
look	
see	
sit	

Letter patterns

RESOURCE SHEET 5

Name _____

This is a pattern of letters made from Libby Martin's name. Copy them and then make patterns from the letters in your name.

LILILILILILILILILILILILI

MmMmMmMmMmMmMmM

Opposites

<u>RESOURCE SHEET 6</u>

Name _____

Find the opposite word for all these words:

hot	
wet	
good	
pull	
on	
day	
yes	
slowly	
stop	
over	

Writing a letter

RESOURCE SHEET 7

Name _____

Write a letter to your friend.

Writing a letter

Getting dressed

RESOURCE SHEET 8

Name _____

Draw clothes on this boy.

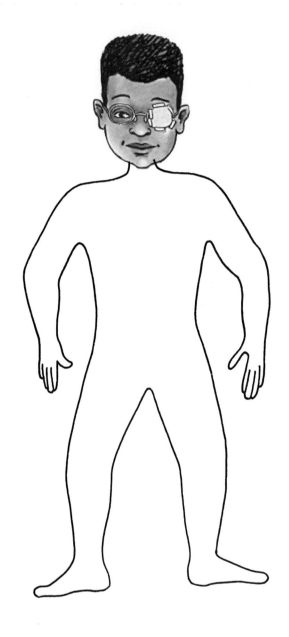

52

Libby Martin

RESOURCE SHEET 9

Name _____

What is Libby saying?

Libby and Sam

RESOURCE SHEET 10

Name _____

Draw a line from each Libby to Sam. Keep inside the tracks.

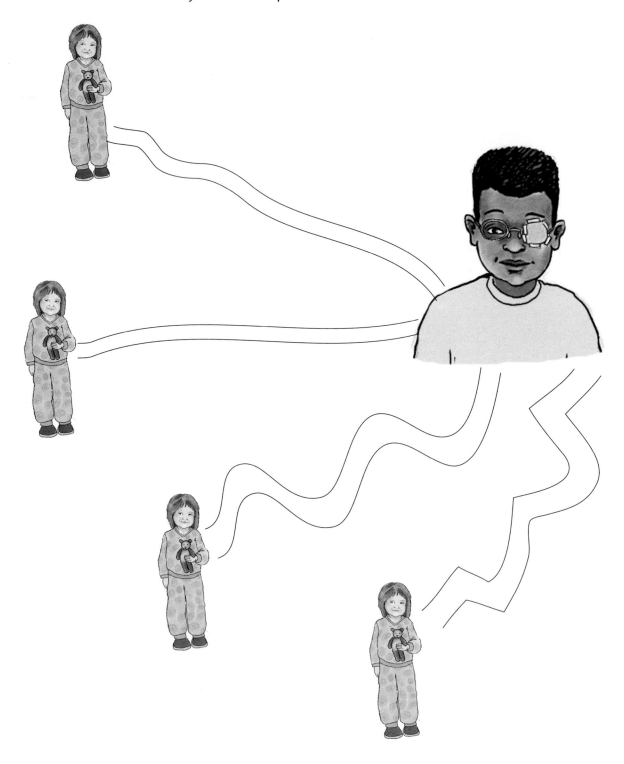